Critical Thinking and Policing

Critical Thinking and Policing

Mathias Okoi-Uyouyo
Abdul M. Sulaiman

Bookman Publishers
Ntoe Asi Odo Street
Parliamentary Extension
Calabar, Nigeria
Tel: +234-807-938-8706
E-mail: bookmanpublishers@gmail.com

ISBN 979-870-456-687-8
(Amazon paperback)

Cover design by Isiaka Gbodiyan
Cover photo by Destiny Abah

CONTENTS

FOREWORD

I feel highly honoured to be asked to write the foreword of this landmark book, written by an accomplished writer and public servant, Mathias Okoi-Uyouyo, and an equally brilliant police officer and academic, DCP Abdul M. Sulaiman.

After a career in the Nigeria Police Force, spanning over 30 years and retiring as an Inspector-General of Police, and recently called out of retirement after 17 years to head the Police Service Commission, which has oversight functions over the Force, I believe I am well placed to confirm the unique importance of this book to police officers in particular, other law enforcement agents, and the public in general.

The book *Critical Thinking and Policing* fills a void in policing literature. It gives police officers the opportunity to learn virtually all that they need to know to be effective in policing. The book not only speaks to critical thinking and policing, but also to day-to-day police work.

The underlying issues of critical thinking in training, criminal investigation, intelligence analysis, police operations and decision making, as examined in the book, are *sine qua non* from the beginning to the end of every police career. I foresee the book playing a vital role in properly preparing police officers and law enforcement officials at all levels. I therefore have no hesitation in strongly recommending the book to all and sundry.

Musiliu A. K. Smith, IGP (Rtd.), CFR, FNIM, fwc
Chairman, Police Service Commission

January, 2020

INTRODUCTION

Crime is a dynamic phenomenon and has evolved from the rudimentary and simplistic form into a complex enterprise. Underlining this transition is the subject of technological advancement (especially information technology), legal development, political evolution, economic complexities and social factors, all of which have combined to shape human conduct and open up new opportunities for the conceptualisation, planning and perfection of crime.

The import of this is that policing across the world must of necessity also evolve in line with the dynamics of crime. As such, from the *hue and cry* policing model, modern police-driven law enforcement activities is increasingly guided by the need to engage proficient application of intellect in the dissection of crimes.

In essence, crime governance in the 21st Century has gone beyond the hue and cries, application of brute force, and archaic approaches. It now demands a more complex usage of strategic police management tools. This trend requires that every police officer must acquire, develop and apply the power of critical thinking to all police challenges that they routinely confront in the performance of their functions.

Indeed, it could be safely asserted that the level of efficiency of any Police Force today depends fundamentally on the critical thinking capabilities of its strategic managers whose responsibility it is to provide requisite quality professional leadership that will shape the conduct of all subordinates within the policing system.

Beneath this assertion also is that even the junior ranking police officer that Lanni and Lanni in their book *Street Cops and Management Cops* (published in 1983 by the MIT Press, Cambridge), refer to as the *street cops* who interact on constant basis directly with members of the public as well as engage criminal elements in lethal, life threatening combats based on split seconds decisions equally need to acquire the elements of critical thinking to guide them in reacting to such situations. It is in this context that this publication is seen as of critical importance to modern policing.

The book engages in a critical discourse on how to improve and cultivate critical thinking capabilities; the importance of inclusion and usage of critical thinking in police training; application of critical thinking to criminal investigation; the pivotal role of critical thinking in intelligence analysis; and critical thinking in aid of police operations and decision making in policing activities.

The uniqueness of the publication lies in the fact that the authors made their research relative to the Nigerian policing environment while equally drawing on global perspectives in arriving at their conclusions. The book is, therefore, an invaluable intellectual and professional contribution to the discourse on policing in Nigeria, in particular and across the world, in general.

The distinctiveness of the publication also lies in the fact that the authors deviate from the dominant research focus on police studies in Nigeria and open a new field of knowledge and, perhaps, debate on the relationship between strategic police management and police operational efficiency. The book will essentially be of inestimable value not only to serving police officers and other law enforcement agents, but also to students, researchers, and policy makers with bias for police studies. I therefore commend the authors for their foresight, intellectual depth, and for contributing to field of knowledge in this form.

In recommending the publication as a guide to strategic police managers and other law enforcement agents in Nigeria and beyond, I encourage students of policing to take advantage of the broad-based body of knowledge that the publication advances towards enriching their academic profiles.

Mohammed A. Adamu, NPM, mni
Inspector-General of Police
Federal Republic of Nigeria

December, 2019

PREFACE

This book is about thinking, thinking critically. It is also about policing. Thinking critically is one skill that is required of every police officer; it is one of the most critical assets of policing. The greatest advancements in tackling crimes have come from ideas, ideas that are borne from critical thinking.

Critical thinking helps in investigation, appraisal, decision making and problem solving. These are activities police officers encounter daily in the course of their work. It is a skill that can be acquired and improved upon. This is what has formed the focus of this book.

This book has also set out to teach us – how police officers can acquire thinking skills; how to improve their capacity to think critically; how to improve their capacity to reason; and how they can apply it to policing, decision making and problem solving.

Mathias Okoi-Uyouyo
Abdul M. Sulaiman

December, 2019

ACKNOWLEDGEMENTS

In 2017, we were saddled with the responsibility of setting up a presidential investigation panel as Director of Administration and Director of Operations. The job entailed drawing personnel from different law enforcement and compliance agencies, as well as the public service to achieve the panel's objectives. The period coincided with the thesis writing phase of Abdul M. Sulaiman at the University of Abuja, where he was pursuing a Ph.D. His thesis was on *Critical Thinking and Learning Styles among Nigeria Police Force Training Institutions*. Although we left in the first quarter of 2018 for higher responsibilities, the idea for this book was sown. We are grateful for this experience, which set the foundation for this book.

We wish to specially thank the following police, military and intelligence officers, serving and retired, for their invaluable insights: Musiliu A. K. Smith, Parry Osayande, M. D. Abubakar, Sulaiman Abba, Solomon Arase, Mohammed A. Adamu, Gabriel Edmund Okoi, Salihu Argungu, Abbati Dikko, Anthony Ogbizi, Sani Mohammed, Abdul Dahiru Danwawu, Nuhu Ribadu, Farida Waziri, Ibrahim Lamorde, Ibrahim Magu, Ede Ayuba, Omini Okoi Akpabi, and Uket Iwara.

ACKNOWLEDGEMENTS

We are also grateful to Zanna Mohammed Ibrahim, Moses Jitoboh, Dan-Mallam Mohammed, Joseph Egbunike, Sadiq I. Abubakar, Peter Wagbara, Isyaku Mohammed, Okoi Akpama, Umar Ali Fagge, Tony Emefile, Salihu Ishaq, Adamu Elleman, Mohammed Guri, Emmanuel Asufi, Ofem Arikpo, Usman Tahir, Ime Udofia, Salihu Khan and Hammanjoda Barka.

Thanks to Kalu Uka, Rabiu Abdullahi, Maurice Archibong, and Ayator Datsu who read the manuscript and made valuable suggestions; and to J. B. Badu and H. A. Apeh, who had earlier supervised the doctoral thesis of Abdul M. Sulaiman for their valued comments.

We would also like to acknowledge the following persons, for their encouragement and support: Seriake Dickson, Goddy Jedy Agba, Festus Keyamo, Ebose Augustine Osegha, Eteng Jones Williams, Hamza Sule Wuro Bokki, Lawrence Alobi, E. E. Amedu, Ernest Ibazi, Comfort Obi, Austin Braimoh, Umoh Eka, Tijani Mohammed, Bello Balarabe Gusau, Bashir Umar, Kammonke Abam, Ubi Otu Eno, Iwara U. Iwara, Ibor Inah, Rose Uyouyo Okoi, Inyang Okoi Uyouyo, Azimi Abdul, Musa Abdul, Mohammed Abdul and Tahir Abdul.

Finally, we pay tribute to members of our family for enduring our absence during the course of the book, and sustaining the atmosphere that enabled us to complete the work – Glory and the boys: Jersam and Wofai (Mathias Okoi-Uyouyo); as well as Jamila, Fatima, Samira, Safiya, Khadija, Faisal, Abdulsalam, Maryam, Noor, Sabiha and Sabira (Abdul M. Sulaiman).

THE CONCEPT OF CRITICAL THINKING AND POLICING

Critical Thinking

It is difficult to answer the question: What is critical thinking? The main reason being that its definition is highly contestable due to divergent notions of the concept. This lack of a common definition has also contributed to its poor understanding and usage. Philosophers, educationists and psychologists have all attempted to construct their own views of the concept, leading to incomplete views instead of a greater insight. However, a history and definition of critical thinking is the first step to understanding its relevance to policing.

The intellectual roots of critical thinking date back to Socrates, who developed a method of probing questioning that forced people to justify their confident claims to knowledge. Socrates established that one cannot depend upon those 'in authority' to have sound knowledge and insight. He demonstrated that persons may have power and high position and yet be confused and irrational. He established the importance of asking probing questions before we accept ideas as being worthy of belief. His method of questioning is now known as 'Socratic questioning', and is the best known critical thinking strategy.[1]

Socrates set the agenda for the tradition of critical thinking, namely, to reflectively question common beliefs and explanations, carefully distinguishing those beliefs that are reasonable and logical from those which – however appealing – lack adequate evidence or rational foundation to warrant our belief.[2]

Socrates was followed by the critical thinking of Plato (who recorded Socrates' thoughts), Aristotle, and the Greek sceptics, all of whom emphasised that things are often very different from what they appear to be and that only the trained mind is prepared to see through their essence.[3]

In the Middle Ages, the tradition of systematic critical thinking was embodied in the writings and teachings of such thinkers as Thomas Aquinas (*Sumna Theologica*). To ensure his thinking met the test of critical thought, Aquinas systematically stated, considered, and answered all criticisms of his ideas as a necessary stage in developing them. During the Renaissance (15th and 16th centuries), a flood of scholars in Europe began to think critically about religion, art, society, human nature, law, and freedom. They followed up on the insight of the ancients.[4]

The earliest use of the critical thinking as an educational goal dates back to 1910 when the American philosopher, John Dewey, who had referred to it as 'reflective thinking' defined it as "active, persistent and careful consideration of any belief or supposed form of knowledge in the light of the grounds that support it, and the further conclusions to which it tends"[5]. It is the practice of "making informed evaluative judgements about claims and arguments"; with its main features as: "analysis (interpretation), evaluation and further argument"; and characterised by being "fair and open-minded; active and informed; sceptical and independent".[6]

Three features have been identified as making up critical thinking: if it is done for the purpose of making up one's mind about what to believe or do; if the person engaging in the thinking is trying to fulfil standards of adequacy and accuracy appropriate to the thinking; and if the thinking fulfils the relevant standards to some threshold level.[7] A breakdown of these features reflects a goal-oriented thinking.

Critical thinking is an essential and vital component of modern policing. It is the wish of police officers that they and their colleagues have it, for with it, one can think correctly on how to solve problems.

A person who thinks critically can ask appropriate questions, gather relevant information, efficiently and creatively sort through this information, reason logically from this information, and come to reliable and trustworthy conclusions about the world that enabled one to live and act successfully in it.[8]

There is a clear distinction between critical thinking and survival-level thinking. Critical thinking is higher-order thinking. One does not need to think critically to take a decision on his or her own survival. Even children after birth nurture the capabilities on how to survive. Human beings are not born with the capability to think critically. It is learned, and it is not every human being that was born that gets to learn it.

Critical thinking also involves inquiry – the ability to ask questions and provide answers that challenge established dogmas, the ability to query traditional beliefs. Such skills are germane in problem solving, and that is why critical thinking skills can also be defined as problem-solving skills – skills that enable us make decisions that we can be held responsible for about situations and life, taking into account the consequences of such decisions. When we scrutinise a thought to transform it for the best possible option, we are thinking critically. It is the focused direction of thought.

Critical thinking is purposeful, directed thought. It is not easy, as it requires explicit mental energy. The great majority of the decisions and issues we face throughout the day do not require critical thinking. The route we drive to work, what clothes we wear to a party, and what book to read on Saturday are examples of decisions or concerns that do not normally require critical thinking and can be made in an "automatic" mode of cognitive thought.[9]

The "critical" part of critical thinking denotes an evaluation component. Sometimes the word "critical" is used to convey something "negative and fault-finding", as when we say "She is a critical person." However, evaluation can and should be a constructive reflection of positive and negative attributes. When we think critically, we are evaluating the outcomes of our thought process – the reasoning that went into the conclusion we have arrived at or the kinds of factors considered in making a decision.[10]

Critical also means "involving or exercising skilled judgement or observation." In this sense, critical thinking means thinking clearly and intelligently. More precisely, critical thinking is the general term given to a wide range of cognitive skills and intellectual dispositions needed to effectively identify, analyse, and evaluate truth and claims; to discover and overcome personal preconceptions and biases; to formulate and present convincing reasons in support of conclusions; and to make reasonable, intelligent decisions about what to believe and what to do. It is disciplined thinking governed by clear intellectual standards.[11]

Policing

One of the most widely known and most misunderstood of public institutions is the police. The Nigeria Police Force suffers the same fate. To the average citizen, the police is all about law enforcement, 'catching criminals' and protecting us from crime. But the police is much more than that. It is an organisation that performs a wide-range of roles, making the popular depiction of limiting policing to crime-fighting quite misleading. Law enforcement accounts for only a small percentage of police work. For instance, maintenance of order and other wide range of activities that the police performs and which takes more time and resources do not relate to law enforcement, but all contribute to crime control and law enforcement.

Although often treated as synonymous, police and policing need to be understood as distinct concepts. Policing relates to broad processes of social regulation that underpin the routines of everyday life, as such, these are performed by a wide range of agencies and institutions.[12]

History of the Police in Nigeria

The history of the police in Nigeria dates back to the inception of colonial rule in 1861, when the British colonisers established police forces for the conquered territories to protect them against the revolts of indigenous people. This saw the establishment of several police forces for the Lagos Colony, Niger Coast and the Northern and Southern Protectorates. Native Authorities and local government police forces were also established from 1916 onwards, under the control of the traditional rulers in the Northern and Western parts of the country.[13] This arrangement was a reflection of the indirect rule system, which vested certain administrative functions on the traditional institutions.

The Native Authority Ordinance (No. 4 of 1916) conferred on the Native Authorities the responsibility for maintaining order in their respective areas. Under it, they were allowed to prevent crime and arrest offenders by employing 'any person' to assist them in carrying out their police duties. Their police powers were [further] increased under the Protectorate Laws (Enforcement) Ordinance (No. 15 of 1924).[14]

Under the colonial laws, the *akodas* who served as palace messengers of the Yoruba kings and the *dogarai* who performed similar roles for the Emirs in the North were reorganised to form the local police forces – *olopas* and *'yan doka*. The colonial administration also established the Northern and Southern Police Forces between 1900 – 1930. In 1930, the Nigeria Police Force was created by the merger of the Northern and Southern Police Forces. Both the Nigeria Police Force, the local administration police forces of the local government areas in Western Nigeria and the Native Authorities of Northern Nigeria continued to co-exist until 1966 when the local forces were disbanded by the military regime of Major General J.T.U. Aguiyi-Ironsi, leaving only the federal police force.

The Aguiyi-Ironsi regime had set up the Yusuf Gobir Panel to consider the desirability of dual (local and federal) police and prison forces. The Panel in its *Working Party Report on the Police and Prisons* submitted in 1967 noted that: The local police forces were poorly trained, corrupt and used for partisan political purposes, including the repression of opponents by traditional rulers and politicians in Northern Nigeria, as well as by political parties and governments in power in the Northern and Western Regions.[15]

The Nigeria Police Force as presently constituted is derived from section 214 of the 1999 constitution which provides for its establishment when it came into effect:

> There shall be a Police Force for Nigeria, which shall be known as the Nigeria Police Force.[16]

It further provides that:

> Subject to the provisions of this section, no other Police Force shall be established for the Federation or any part thereof.[17]

Duties of the Nigeria Police Force

The organisation, establishment, administration, duties and powers of the Force are all creations of the law. Unless a duty or power is prescribed or considered by law, such duty is not obligatory nor is the power excisable by the police, as the constitution also makes pronouncements regarding its duties and powers in section 214 (2) (b) "The members of the Nigeria Police shall have such powers and duties as may be conferred upon them by law".[18]

The Police Act in Part II section 4 states the general duties of the Force as:

> The police shall be employed for the prevention and detection of crime, the apprehension of offenders, the preservation of law and order; the protection of life and property and the due enforcement of all laws and regulations with which they are directly charged, and shall perform such military duties within or without Nigeria as may be required of them by, or under the authority of this or any other act.[19]

2

HOW TO IMPROVE ON CRITICAL THINKING

Becoming a skilled thinker requires practice. Everyone 'practices' thinking, but the question is whether he or she is practising good or bad habits.[1] The simple action of thinking does not translate to becoming a more and more skilled thinker with time.

Critical thinking is comparable to most of the things we face in life: What you put into a situation determines its outcomes. It can be a worthwhile and life-changing experience, when approached as a chance to learn habits of disciplined thinking that are critical to success as a police officer and in life.

Developing as a critical thinker requires an understanding and practising of thinking skills. This is what would make one evaluate if they are improving or not, by judging performance against a meaningful set of quality standards. Thinking, like every other skillset, requires instructions in both the attributes (skills involved) and measures of success (quality measures).[2]

It is not enough to only know the skills needed for critical thinking. To be successful, analysts as critical thinkers also need certain attitudes, dispositions, passions, and traits of mind.[3] Actively thinking critically hones the skills; practice yields proficiency. But in order to gain mastery, willingness to reason in this manner becomes essential.[4]

Critical thinking is more than just the accumulation of facts and knowledge; it is the methodology used in finding answers to whatever is occupying one's mind to arrive at the best possible conclusions.

Critical thinkers have certain characteristics. To improve on critical thinking, one needs to develop those characteristics. Patel (2018) identified sixteen characteristics of critical thinkers.[5]

Characteristics of Critical Thinkers

Observation

Observation is one of the earliest critical thinking skills we learn as children – it is our ability to perceive and understand the world around us. Careful observation includes our ability to document details, and to collect data through our senses. Our observations eventually lead to insight and a deeper understanding of the world.

Curiosity

Curiosity is a core trait of many successful leaders. Being inherently inquisitive and interested in the world and people around you is a hallmark of leaders who are critical thinkers. Instead of taking everything at face value, a curious person will wonder why something is the way it is.

As we get older, it is easier to put aside what may seem like childish curiosity. Curiosity forces you to keep an open mind and propels you to gain deeper knowledge – all of which are also fundamental to being a lifelong learner.

Objectivity

Good critical thinkers are able to stay as objective as possible when looking at information or a situation. They focus on facts, and on the scientific evaluation of the information at hand. Objective thinkers seek to keep their emotions (and those of others) from affecting their judgement.

However, it is impossible for people to remain completely objective, because we are all shaped by our points of view, our life experiences, and our perspectives. Being aware of our biases is the first step to being objective and looking at an issue dispassionately. Once you are able to remove yourself from the situation, you can more thoroughly analyse it.

Introspection

This is the art of being aware of your thinking – or, to put it in another way, thinking about how you think about things. Critical thinkers need introspection so they are aware of their own degree of alertness and attentiveness, as well as their biases. This is your ability to examine your innermost thoughts, feelings and sensations. Introspection is closely related to self-reflection, which gives you insight into your emotional and mental state.

Analytical Thinking

The best analytical thinkers are also critical thinkers, and vice versa. The ability to analyse information is key when looking at almost anything, whether it is a contract, report, business model or even a relationship.

Analysing information means to break information down to its component parts and evaluate how well those parts function together and separately. Analysis relies on observation; on gathering and evaluating evidence so you can come to a meaningful conclusion. Analytical thinking begins with objectivity.

Identifying Biases

Critical thinkers challenge themselves to identify the evidence that forms their beliefs and assess whether or not those sources are credible. Doing this helps you understand your own biases and question your preconceived notions. This is an important step in becoming aware of how biases intrude on your thinking and recognising when information may be skewed.

When looking at information, ask yourself: Who does the information benefits? Does the source of this information have an agenda? Does the source overlook or leave out information that does not support its claims or beliefs?

Determining Relevance

One of the most difficult parts of thinking critically is figuring out what information is the most relevant, meaningful and important for your consideration. In many scenarios, you will be presented with information that may seem valuable, but it may turn out to be only a minor data point to consider.

Consider whether or not a source of information is logically relevant to the issue being discussed. Is it truly useful and unbiased, or is it merely distracting from a more pertinent point?

Inference

Information does not always come with a summary that spells out exactly what it means. Critical thinkers need to assess the information and draw conclusions based on raw data. Inference is the ability to extrapolate meaning from data and discover potential outcomes when assessing a scenario.

It is also important to understand the difference between inference and assumptions. For example, if you see data that someone weighs 260 pounds, you might assume they are overweight or unhealthy. However, other data points like height and body composition may alter that conclusion.

Compassion and Empathy

Having compassion and empathy may seem like a negative for critical thinkers. After all, being sentimental and emotional can skew our perception of a situation. But the point of having compassion is to have concern for others and to value the welfare of other people.

Without compassion, we would view all information and situations from the viewpoint of cold, heartless, scientific facts and data. It would be easy to allow our cynicism to become toxic, and to be suspicious of everything we look at. But to be a good critical thinker, we must always take into account the human element. Not everything we do is about detached data and information – it is also about people.

Humility

Humility is the willingness to acknowledge one's shortcomings and see one's positive attributes in an accurate way. When you have humility, you are aware of your flaws, but also your strengths, and this is an important element in critical thinking and being willing to stretch and open your mind.

When you have intellectual humility, you are open to other people's viewpoints, you recognise when you are wrong and you are willing to challenge your own beliefs when necessary.

Willingness to Challenge the Status Quo

Critical thinking means questioning long-established practices and refusing to adhere to traditional methods simply because that is the way it has always been done. Critical thinkers are looking for smart, well-thought out answers and methods that take into account all the current and relevant information and practices available. Their willingness to challenge the status quo may seem controversial, but it is an essential part of the creative and innovative mind of a critical thinker.

Open-Mindedness

Being able to step back from a situation and not become embroiled helps critical thinkers see the broader view. Critical thinkers avoid launching into a frenzied argument or taking sides – they want to hear all perspectives. Critical thinkers do not jump to conclusions. They approach a question or situation with an open mind and embrace other opinions and views.

Awareness of Common Thinking Errors

Critical thinkers do not allow their logic and reasoning to become clouded by illusions and misconceptions. They are aware of common logical fallacies, which are errors in reasoning that often creep into arguments and debates. Some common errors in thinking include:

- Circular reasoning, in which the premise of an argument or a conclusion is used as support for the argument itself.
- Cognitive shortcut bias, in which you stubbornly stick to a favoured view or argument when other more effective possibilities or explanations exist.
- Confusing correlation with causation. In other words, asserting that when two things happen together, one causes the

other. Without direct evidence, this assumption is not justified.

Creative Thinking

Effective critical thinkers are also largely creative thinkers. Creative thinkers reject standardised formats for problem solving – they think outside the box. They have a wide range of interests and adopt multiple perspectives on a problem. They are also open to experimenting with different methods and considering different viewpoints.

The biggest difference between critical thinkers and creative thinkers is that creativity is associated with generating ideas, while critical thinking is associated with analysing and appraising those ideas. Creativity is important to bringing in novel ideas; critical thinking can bring those ideas into clearer focus.

Effective Communicators

In many cases, problems with communication are based on an inability to think critically about a situation or see it from different perspectives. Effective communication starts with a clear thought process.

Critical thinking is the tool we use to coherently build our thoughts and express them. Critical thinking relies on following another person's thought process and line of reasoning. An effective critical thinker must be able to relay his or her ideas in a compelling way and then absorb the responses of others.

Active Listeners

Critical thinkers do not just want to get their point across to others; they are also careful to engage in active listening and really hear others' points of view. Instead of being a passive listener during a conversation or discussion, they actively try to participate.

Asking questions to help them distinguish facts from assumptions is a major attribute of critical thinkers. They gather information and seek to gain insight by asking open-ended questions that probe deeper into the issue.

Bassham, et al. (2011), offer a general profile of a critical thinker by contrasting some of the key intellectual traits of critical thinkers with the relevant traits of uncritical thinkers.[6]

Critical Thinkers …	*Uncritical Thinkers …*
Have a passionate drive for clarity, precision, accuracy, and other critical thinking standards.	Often think in ways that are unclear, imprecise, and inaccurate.
Are sensitive to ways in which critical thinking can be skewed by egocentrism, sociocentrism, wishful	Often fall prey to egocentrism, sociocentrism, relativistic thinking, unwarranted assumptions, and

thinking, and other impediments.	wishful thinking.
Are skilled at understanding, analysing, and evaluating arguments and viewpoints.	Often misunderstand or evaluate arguments and viewpoints unfairly.
Reason logically and draw appropriate conclusions from evidence and data.	Think illogically and draw unsupported conclusions from evidence and data.
Are intellectually honest with themselves, acknowledging what they do not know and recognising their limitations.	Pretend they know more than they do and ignore their limitations.
Listen open-mindedly to opposing points of view and welcome criticisms of beliefs and assumptions.	Are closed-minded and resist criticisms of beliefs and assumptions.
Base their beliefs on facts and evidence rather than on personal preference or self-interest.	Often base beliefs on mere personal preference or self-interest.
Are aware of the biases and pre-conceptions that shape the way they perceive the world.	Lack awareness of their own biases and preconceptions.
Think independently and are not afraid to disagree with group opinion.	Tend to engage in "group-think," uncritically following the beliefs and values of the crowd.
Are able to get to the heart of an issue or a problem, without being distracted by details.	Are easily distracted and lack the ability to zero in on the essence of an issue or a problem.

Have the intellectual courage to face and assess fairly ideas that challenge even their most basic beliefs.

Fear and resist ideas that challenge their basic beliefs.

Pursue truth and are curious about a wide range of issues.

Are often relatively indifferent to truth and lack curiosity.

Have the intellectual perseverance to pursue insights or truths despite obstacles or difficulties.

Tend not to persevere when they encounter intellectual obstacles or difficulties.

Models on How to Improve on Critical Thinking

There are quite a number of models on how to think critically. For the purpose of this book, the four-part model on learning to think critically by Halpern (2014) has been adopted. The model consists of four parts:[7]

1. Explicitly learn the skills of critical thinking.
2. Develop the disposition for effortful thinking and learning.
3. Direct learning activities in ways that increase the probability of transcontextual transfer (structure training).
4. Make metacognitive monitoring explicit and overt.

A Skills Approach to Critical Thinking

The approach recognises generic skills that are important in critical thinking, and which a critical thinker needs to develop. It is based on the postulation that critical thinking instructions are predicated on two assumptions:

(a) that there are evidently distinguishable thinking skills that students can be taught to recognise and apply accordingly, and

(b) that if recognised and applied, the students will be more effective thinkers.

The following generic skills have been identified as important to a critical thinker:

- recognising semantic slanting and guilt by association

- seeking out contradictory evidence

- using the metacognitive knowledge that allows novices to monitor their own performance and to decide when additional help is needed

- making risk benefit assessments

- generating a reasoned method for selecting between several possible courses of actions

- giving reasons for choices as well as varying the style and amount of detail in explanations depending on who is receiving the information

- recalling relevant information when it is needed

- using skills for learning new techniques efficiently and relating new knowledge to information that was previously learned
- using numerical information including the ability to think probabilistically and express thoughts numerically
- understanding basic research principles
- demonstrating an advanced ability to read and write complex prose
- presenting a coherent and persuasive argument on a controversial, contemporary topic
- using matrices and other diagrams for communication
- synthesising information from a variety of sources
- determining credibility and using the information in formulating and communicating decisions.

The Disposition for Effortful Thinking and Learning

This method is based on the belief that no one becomes a better thinker if he/she does not put to use the thinking skills they have learnt. It considers growing the outlook or disposition of a critical thinker, as an essential component of critical thinking. It is also based on the conviction that good thinkers are driven to wield efforts required to work in a planful manner, double-check for correctness, gather information, and carry on when the solution is not apparent.

Another theory of the disposition for effortful thinking and learning is that many errors occur, not because people cannot think critically, but because they do not think. It identifies the disposition or attitudes critical thinkers exhibit as follows:

- willingness to plan
- flexibility
- persistence
- willingness to self-correct, admit errors, and change mind when the evidence changes
- being mindful, and
- consensus-seeking.

Structure/Transfer of Training

Having a wide range of critical thinking skills and willingness to apply them in the effortful process they will be used has been identified as germane to becoming a better thinker. The third component of the four-part model on learning to think critically includes identifying when critical thinking is needed so one can chose the most suitable skill for the situation. It focuses on the need for critical thinkers to recollect clues from the structural parts of the problem or argument in order that, when the structural parts are present, they will be able to serve as clues for retrieval.

The model drawing from the old saying in psychology that "the head remembers what it does," advocates for the direction of one's learning so that, critical thinking skills are learned in a way that will enable recollection in unique circumstances. It gives examples of thinking tasks, designed to assist with the transfer of critical thinking skills. The tasks, which attract attention to structural parts of the problem or argument, require learners to centre on the structural parts of the problems, in order to identify and use an appropriate critical thinking skill:

- Draw a diagram or other graphic display that organises the information.
- List additional information you would want before answering a question.
- Explain why a particular multiple-choice alternative was selected. Which is second best? Why?
- State the problem in at least two ways.
- Identify which information is most important. Which information is least important? Why?
- Categorise the findings in a meaningful way.
- List two solutions for each problem.

- Identify what is wrong with an assertion that was made in the question.
- Present two reasons that support the conclusion and two reasons that do not support the conclusion.
- Identify the type of persuasive technique being used.
- Present two actions you would take to improve the design of a study that was described.

Metacognitive Monitoring

Metacognition is the awareness, and understanding of one's own thought processes, thinking, and knowledge. It is the knowledge of what we know, and its application to learning activities. It is the thinking 'about' thinking.

When engaging in critical thinking, one needs to observe his or her own thinking process, check whether or not there is progress in the direction of a suitable objective, maintain accuracy, and make choices about the use of time and rational effort.

Metacognition denotes in-depth thinking in which thought processes involved in learning are actively controlled. This includes planning how to get a given learning task done, monitoring understanding, and estimating progress toward the completion of a task.[8]

3

IMPORTANCE OF CRITICAL THINKING IN POLICE TRAINING

Scholars have advocated for the inclusion of learning critical thinking skills and disposition in the curriculum of police officer's training, where there is none, in view of its importance to policing. One of the objectives of police education and training is to produce officers with the aptitude to think critically.[1] The degree of success for an officer with critical thinking skills and disposition in the profession is highly probable.

In the course content of the Law Enforcement Basic Training Curriculum, prepared by the Training and Standards Bureau, Wisconsin Department of Justice, critical thinking and decision making constitutes a major part. During the course, trainees are taught a structured approach to problem solving and decision making. This structured approach uses critical thinking skills and processes, which officers can use in the resolution of a wide-range of problems. The course lay emphases on the thinking and problem solving process, not on having the right or wrong answer to a problem. The objective of the course is to help trainees develop the following competencies:

- Analyse different methods used to make decisions.
- Recognise factors that influence decision making.
- Explain expectations regarding law enforcement decisions.
- Describe pitfalls or traps when making decisions.
- Enhance an officer's critical thinking and police problem solving abilities.[2]

A lot of skills are of utmost importance in policing. These skills are quite numerous and include critical thinking. Police training should be structured to inculcate these skills that would be beneficial to the officers in the job, even though much is learned while in it.

Critical thinking is an unwavering and sceptical frame of mind that always checks for accuracy, and searches for potential flaws in the argument. It is an area that forensic science, because of its adherence to the scientific method, focuses on, but most times police officers do not get the same education. Officers have to be trained on how to look for the flaws in their evidence and reasoning during an investigation and make every effort to avoid validation of bias.[3]

When police officers charge a person with a crime, they are required to gather probable cause. Probable cause means they must gather evidence that creates a reasonable belief the offender committed the crime. Officers principally make an argument that the suspect violated a particular statute, and that argument is then subjected to further scrutiny by prosecutors, judges, and ultimately a jury. The entire process is based on forming sound arguments. The consequence of not forming a sound argument could translate to possibly imprisoning the wrong person or arriving at a wrong conclusion about the situation. Officers must have well-honed critical thinking skills in order to come to a sound conclusion and then make an incontrovertible argument. Concentrating on critical thinking and report writing during training teaches police officers how to form good arguments and think critically about investigations and evidence. It enables officers to form good arguments, which will make them better, more well-honed and effective officers.[4]

The training atmospheres of most of the police training institutions simulate the military-styled training model for several reasons. Chiefly among them are:

    a. A high-stress model serving as an indoctrination into the police culture.[5]

    b. Creating an environment in which trainees have to prove themselves to the instructors and fellow recruits that they can perform in different situations.[6]

c. Serving as a weeding-out process for those recruits who do not seem to meet the standards of the training institutions.[7]

The thinking behind the high-stress, para-militaristic model is to eliminate individualism and replace it with the mind-set that team processes and shared decision making is vital to the success of being a police officer in the field. It is also this mind-set that permeates the selection process, with priorities given to cadets by police administrators during selection who have the features to adapt to the crime fighter model, obeying orders without hesitation.[8]

The training atmosphere described above is quite inconsistent with what the police officer encounters in the field. Police officers employ individual discretion and critical thinking skills when carrying out their duties. This applies especially in modern-day policing. It is therefore imperative to inculcate the learning of critical thinking skills and disposition in all the instructional manuals run in the police training institutions.

Training models for critical thinking skills for officers have been developed. An example is the cognitive task analysis and critical incident interviews. The training is designed to make the most of both information-based and practice-based training methods. Officers are made to listen to brief verbal presentation of the concepts crucial to the segment, followed by questions and discussions. They are then made to partake in lifelike scenario-based exercises designed to provide practice in the relevant skill, which utilises interactive simulation and feedback provided by group discussions and the instructor.[9] The training content is divided into four segments:[10]

1. An overview of the cycle of creating, testing, and evaluating stories to improve situation understanding.
2. A particular kind of story based on hostile intent.
3. Strategies for handling conflicting evidence and for generating alternate interpretations of evidence.
4. Guidelines for deciding when critical thinking is appropriate and when immediate action is necessary.

The training strategy is called critical thinking because it is designed for situations where familiar patterns or rules do not fit. The four training segments are as follows:[11]

- *Creating, Testing and Evaluating Stories.* This section provides an overview of the critical thinking process, called *STEP*. When an assessment is uncertain, decision makers take it seriously by constructing a story around it. The story includes the past, present, and future events that would be expected if the assessment were true. Decision makers use the story to test the assessment, by matching prospects to what is known or observed. When evidence appears to conflict with the assessment, they try to patch up the story by explaining the evidence. They then evaluate the result; if the patched up story involves too many unreliable assumptions, they create alternate assessments and begin the cycle again. In the time being, they plan against the possibility that their current best story is wrong.

- *Hostile-Intent Stories.* Stories contain certain typical components. Knowledge of these components can help decision makers notice and fill gaps in the stories they construct. A specific and significant sort of story is built around the assessment of hostile intent. The training teaches officers by practice and example how to discover story components and to let the stories guide them to appropriate evidence about intent.

- *Critiquing Stories.* After a story is created, decision makers step back and evaluate its believability. This segment of the training introduces a devil's advocate technique for uncovering hidden assumptions in a story and generating alternative interpretations of the evidence. An infallible crystal ball persistently tells the decision maker that the current assessment is wrong, despite the evidence that seems to support it, and asks for an explanation of that evidence. Irrespective of how assured decision makers are in their assessments, this technique can effectively alert them to notable options. It can also help them see how conflicting data could fit into a story. In each case, the technique helps decision makers expose and evaluate assumptions underlying their reading of the evidence.

- *When to Think More.* Critical thinking is not always appropriate. Unless three conditions are satisfied, the decision maker should probably act immediately: (1) The risk of delay must be acceptable. (2) The cost of an error if one acts immediately must be high. And (3) the situation must be non-routine or problematic in some way. Training focuses on the way experienced decision makers apply these criteria. For example, they tend to utilise more precise estimates of how much time is available, based on the specifics of the situation. They adopt a longer-term outlook in estimating the costs of an error. And they show greater sensitivity to the mismatch between the situation and familiar patterns.

Critical thinking skills and disposition have been established to play an important role in policing. Training in critical thinking will increase the accurateness of the assessment of police officers in the field, which will also impact positively on their confidence and performance. Training officers in such skills and disposition is undeniably a valued addition to effective policing.

4

APPLICATION OF CRITICAL THINKING TO INVESTIGATION

One of the most testing features of modern-day policing is the ease with which criminals have access to advanced technology, making it easier for them to plot and commit crimes. To equal the level of increasing sophistication in criminal activities, policing has to go a notch higher in its investigations. This has made the use of critical thinking skills in criminal investigations more imperative.

In the case of Chief Gani Fawehinmi v. Inspector-General of Police, Commissioner of Police, Lagos and Nigeria Police Force, the Supreme Court affirmed the powers of the police to investigate crime. Delivering judgement, S. O. Uwaifo J.S.C. said:

> The *1999 Constitution* recognises one police force for Nigeria and the said police are given a duty under section 4 of the Police Act [now in Cap. 359, Laws of the Federation of Nigeria, 1990] to prevent and detect crime, apprehend offenders,

35

preserve law and order, protect life and property and enforce all laws and regulations with which they are directly charged, and that it is an important statutory duty which they owe to the generality of Nigerians and all other persons lawfully living in Nigeria. It follows that in their duty to detect crime, allegations of the crime committed by any person should normally be investigated by the police.[1]

Objectives of Criminal Investigation

Virtually every crime calls for a level of investigation. The extent to which the police carry out an investigation is dependent on the availability of resources and how the crime is ranked. However, every investigation is set to achieve certain objectives, chiefly:[2]

- Detect crime.
- Locate and identify suspects in crimes.
- Locate, document, and preserve evidence in crimes.
- Arrest suspects in crimes.
- Recover stolen property.
- Prepare sound criminal cases for prosecution.

Police officers employ a lot of discretion when carrying out investigations to achieve their objectives. Justice S. O. Uwaifo in the judgement of Chief Gani Fawehinmi v. Inspector-General of

Police, Commissioner of Police, Lagos and Nigeria Police Force also reiterated the exercise of discretion by the police:

> But I can see nothing in section 4 of the Police Act which denies them of any discretion whether or not to investigate any particular allegation, or when they decide to investigate to do so to its logical conclusion. The need to exercise a discretion in such a matter may arise from a variety of reasons or circumstances, particularly having regard to the nature of the offences, the resources available, the time and trouble involved and the ultimate end result. It may well be a question of balancing options as well as weighing what is really in the public interest. It is inconceivable that such wide powers and duties of the police must be exercised and performed without any discretion left to responsible police operations. Unless a statute which confers powers or impose duties expressly or by necessary implications excludes the exercise of discretion, or the duty demanded in such that leaves no room for discretion, it is my view that discretionary powers are implied and whenever appropriate, exercised for salutary ends.[3]

The exercise of discretion also calls for the application of critical thinking all through the investigation process. It means taking an in-depth look at what is known and ascertaining what still needs to be known. This is what makes provision for the interrogation of investigative assumptions and initial conclusions.

In critically thinking over what is known and ascertaining what still needs to be known, questions reflecting a range of facts and assumptions are generated. The assumptions may be based on the possible charges that would be brought as a consequence of the investigation. These critical questions might be standard or case specific. Peterson (2005) recommended the following standard questions:[4]

- Who had a motive to commit the crime?
- Who had an opportunity to commit the crime?
- What were the benefits of the crime (money, power, control)?
- Who benefitted from the crime (financially or otherwise)?
- How was the crime committed?
- Where was the crime committed?
- Were weapons involved? If so, what weapons?
- Were vehicles involved? If so, what vehicles?
- Was the crime assisted by technology (computers, pagers, PDAs)?
- Was the crime committed by an individual or a group?
- Was the crime planned or opportunistic?

- What is the modus operandi of the crime?
- Is the modus operandi one used by known criminals?
- Who were the victims of the crime?
- Where did the victims and perpetrators meet?

Critical thinking is vital at every stage of an investigation – from the receipt of the first complaint through getting ready for court. It causes police officers to ask: What is missing? And then leads the work in the direction of filling in the critical gaps in knowledge or preparatory work. It entails continual questioning of the present information and the facts of the case in a manner that lets the police officer to understand actions and actors more accurately.[5]

A good investigator needs to be conscious of his or her-own thinking and that thinking needs to be an intentional process. An investigative process has to be approached using "investigative thinking." Gehl and Plecas (2016) listed five topics, which are the foundation of criminal investigation processes, practices and thinking:[6]

1. Criminal investigation as a thinking process.
2. The need to think through the process.
3. Towards modern-day investigation.
4. The path to becoming an investigator.
5. Understanding the investigative mind.

Criminal Investigation as a Thinking Process

Criminal investigation has been described as a multi-faceted, problem-solving challenge. When an officer arrives at a crime scene, he or she is very so often expected to promptly make critical decisions, based on inadequate information, in changing environs of active and still developing events, which sometimes involves life and death. After the occurrence of the criminal incident, the investigating police officer is expected to preserve the crime scene, assemble the evidence, and develop an investigative plan that will lead to the establishment of convincing grounds to detect and apprehend the individual or individuals responsible for the crime.

Criminal investigation is not just a set of task skills; it is in the same way a set of thinking skills. To turn out to be an effective police investigator, these skills must be determinedly understood and developed to a degree where they are purposefully used to work through the criminal investigation process.

The Need to Think Through the Process

Every investigating police officer is required to critically evaluate all the information they come across in the course of an investigation. The reason for this is that, every investigation is a process they can be held responsible. The officer is not just making a resolution of the validity and truth of the information for personal validation of a conviction. Instead, the officer is authorised and empowered by law to make resolutions that might considerably alter the lives of those being investigated as well as the victims of the crime. The interpretation of information and evidence that will lead to those critical decisions, actions and outcomes involve the answering of many questions, such as:

- What must be done to protect the life and safety of persons?
- Should force, up to and including deadly force, be used to resolve a situation?
- Who will become the focus or subject of a criminal investigation?
- What is the best plan to apprehend the person or persons responsible for a criminal act?
- Will someone be subjected to a search of their person or of their home?
- Will someone be subjected to detention or arrest and questioning for a criminal act?
- Will someone have a criminal charge sworn against them?
- Will someone be subjected to a criminal trial?
- Will someone's liberty as a free person be at risk?

- Will justice be served?
- Will the community be protected?

Investigation is the gathering and analysis of evidence. For such evidence to be acceptable in court, the investigating police officer must have both the task and thinking skills to gather and analyse evidence. When on investigating duty, a police officer needs to be in a state of vigilance where he or she can critically evaluate, document, and determine the validity of every piece of information they encounter. In fact, every good investigating police officer has to be intentionally conscious of his or her-own thinking. They must consciously and constantly be mentally engaged and "switched on." Under the "switched on" mode, the investigating police officer must:

- Respond appropriately to situations where they must protect the life and safety of persons.
- Gather the maximum available evidence and information from people and locations.
- Recognise the possible offence or offences being depicted by the fact pattern.
- Preserve and document all evidence and information.
- Critically analyse all available information and evidence.
- Develop an effective investigative plan.

- Strategically act by developing reasonable grounds to both identify and arrest those responsible for criminal acts, or to eliminate those who are wrongfully suspected.

Towards Modern-Day Investigation

Modern-day criminal investigators follow a practice of detecting, gathering and preserving evidence where a person is found committing a criminal act and arrested at the scene; and additional thinking skills of analysis, theory development, and authentication of facts where the suspect is unknown. A wide range of fields are employed to determine how events occurred, and to create an evidence-based fact plan to prove the guiltiness or innocence of an accused.

Forensic science plays a very important role in criminal investigation. Advancements in forensic science have evolved from earlier procedures of identifying suspects and examining physical evidence through physical matching, fingerprints identification and facial recognition systems to connect the accused to victims or to establish guilt or innocence; to modern-day forensic specialities in physical matching, chemical analysis, barefoot morphology, odontology, toxicology, ballistics, biometric analysis, entomology, and DNA analysis. This has greatly enlarged the capacity of forensic experts to detect suspects and scrutinise physical evidences compared to early-years policing.

Specialisation in modern-day fields takes years of training and expertise, but an investigating police officer needs not be proficient in all of them. What the police investigator must strive to attain is an understanding of the available tools, and speciality in their deployment to build the forensic case.

Given the accessibility to a wide range of effective forensic tools, any police officer could find themselves presented with a situation that requires a level of investigative skill. The following skills are essential in how to respond and investigate crime:

- Critical incident response.
- Interpretation of criminal law and offence recognition.
- Crime scene management.
- Evidence identification and preservation.
- Engaging forensic tools for evidence analysis.
- Witness assessment and interviewing.
- Suspect questioning and interrogation.
- Case preparation and documentation.
- Evidence presentation in court.

Furthermore, police officers must have strategic thinking and analytical skills. These higher-level thinking skills have come to be the standard of measurement for capability and competence of investigators. Information technology and forensic science currently play an important role in the justice system, putting more weight on police officers to demonstrate a high-level of capability and competence in them.

The Path to Becoming an Investigator

A professional and proficient investigation by a police officer is all about the tiresome processes of information-gathering and sorting through evidence and facts. It is about excluding options, corroborating events, and documenting evidence, while still engaging in a deliberate process of thinking, evaluating, and purposefully working towards pre-set objectives.

Investigation today has ceased to be the exclusive domain of the police officer; while it used to be in earlier years, it is much less the case today. This change has come as a result of the creation of more law enforcement agencies like the Department of State Services, National Drug Law Enforcement Agency, Federal Roads Safety Commission, Independent Corrupt Practices and other related Offences Commission, Economic and Financial Crimes Commission, Nigeria Security and Civil Defence Corps; and compliance/regulatory agencies like: Police Service Commission, Code of Conduct Bureau, National Human Rights Commission, National Agency for

Food and Drugs Administration and Control, National Agency for the Prohibition of Trafficking in Persons, and the Nigeria Financial Intelligence Unit. What begins as a regulatory abuse can spiral into a criminal conduct. The investigative skills of all law enforcement and compliance/regulatory agencies must also be adept enough to meet the proficiency heights expected of police officers. Certain personal traits tend to be consistent in good investigators. Amongst them are:

- Being passionate about following the facts to discover the truth, with a goal of contributing to the process of justice.
- Being detail-oriented and observant of the facts and the timelines of events.
- Being a flexible thinker, avoiding tunnel vision, and being capable of simultaneously scrutinising different theories while objectively using evidence as the measure to approve or disapprove validity of theories.
- Being patient and capable of maintaining a long-term commitment to reaching a conclusion.
- Being tenacious and not allowing setbacks and false leads to deter continued efforts.
- Being well-informed and skilled at the tasks, process, and procedure while respecting legal authorities and the limitations to take action.

- Being self-aware of bias and intuitive responses, and seeking evidence to support gut-feelings.
- Being trained in the processes of critical thinking that provides reliable analysis of evidence that can later be described and articulated in reports and court testimony.

From the above list of traits, we can accept that, to be a good investigator, one must possess certain attitudes, skills and purposeful thinking processes. All of these form a large chunk of the investigative mind-set. Any person with these traits can work towards growing and refining them to develop into an investigator. Growing the mind-set is a learning process, and the first step in this process is to develop a deliberate awareness of, and engagement in the person's own thinking process.

Understanding the Investigative Mind-Set

This is the personal and organisational conscious-ness to avoid adverse results. It is the safety net against damaging investigative practices e.g. tunnel vision, case ownership and extreme confidentiality. Criminal investigations involve complex thinking to evaluate the validity of information and evidence to guide the investigative process. It is a thinking that develops from suspicion to reasons to believe an arrest should be made, and prosecution in court. This process encompasses a conscious gathering and recording of information to analytical thinking to support the reasons why an arrest should be made and charges pressed. The investigative mind-set involves:

- Disciplined, conscious and control of thinking.
- Being intentionally engaged at a high level of analytical thinking.
- Strategically focused thinking process that prioritises investigative plans and actions to attain results.
- Developing a mental map, and deliberately selecting a path the investigation will follow. This is with the knowledge that the results will only be recognised by court if the reasons for the taken path can be correctly recollected and expressed in detail.

The STAIR Tool and the Investigative Process

The STAIR (situation, tasks, analysis, investigation and results) model is a structured process for strategic investigative response, which can be used by a new investigator to begin the structuring and development of their investigative thinking process. With time and experience, most police investigators learn to structure their thinking, investigative process and response priorities. They learn to build their individual mental roadmaps.[7]

The methods and mental mapping of the STAIR tool used in this book models a process which demonstrates the thinking used by many investigators. It is a tool that can be used by new investigators to structure and develop an investigative thinking process:[8]

SITUATION: Achieving a big picture view of the event to classify and prioritise a response.
- Break out the known facts of the event.
- Offence recognition – identify the possible offence or offences being encountered.
- Offence classification – active event or inactive event.
- Identify all the players – victims, witnesses, and suspects.

TASKS: Focus on the results and the priorities of those results based on even status.
- Tactical investigative response on active event – Level 1: resolve life and safety issues.
- Strategic investigative response on inactive event – Level 2: priorities engaged.
- Crime scene management – evidence identification, evidence preservation, and evidence collection.
- Canvassing for witnesses – witness interviewing.

- Profiling the players – use all police database information – CPIC, PRIME, PROS.
- Document the event – notes, reports, photographs, diagrams and videos.

ANALYSIS: Examine the reported facts, the observed facts, and the physical evidence.

- Make observations and connections between people and circumstances.
- Enhance the meaning of physical evidence by forensic analysis.
- Determine evidence of motive, opportunity, and means to commit the offence.
- Create timelines of activities.
- Develop assumptions and theories that will guide the investigative process.
- Develop investigative plans based on theories.
- Authentication of the event – did it occur at the time, at the place, and in the manner being reported, or is the report a fabrication?

INVESTIGATION: Validating the facts through corroboration of witness accounts and evidence.

- Prioritise the best investigative plans based on most likely theory.

- Test theories against information and evidence discovered through investigation to identify suspects and form reasonable grounds.
- Return to analysis to form new theories or modify theories as new facts are found.

RESULTS: Prioritising and focussing on the results to guide the investigative process.

- Protection of life and safety of people.
- Protection of property.
- Gathering and preserving evidence.
- Accurately documenting the event.
- Establish reasonable grounds to identify and arrest suspects.

5

CRITICAL THINKING AND INTELLIGENCE ANALYSIS

Definitions

To understand the relationship between critical thinking and intelligence analysis, we have to firstly understand the concept of intelligence and analysis.

Intelligence

The word intelligence can be used to describe the process of interpreting information to give it a meaning.[1] It refers to information that meets the stated or understood needs of policymakers.[2] It might also be simply described as processed information. All the same, in law enforcement, "intelligence" could be described as information that is acquired, exploited, and protected by the activities of law enforcement institutions to decide upon and support criminal investigations.[3] All intelligence is information; not all information is intelligence.[4] Intelligence is divided into two main areas:

- *Strategic Intelligence*, which focuses on the long-term aims of law enforcement agencies, and usually reviews current and emerging trends in the crime environment, threats to public safety and order, opportunities for controlling action, and the development of counter programmes and likely avenues for change to policies, programmes and legislation; and

- *Operational Intelligence*, which focuses on the provision of an investigative team with hypotheses and inferences concerning specific elements of illegal operations of any sort. These will include hypotheses and inferences about specific criminal networks, individuals or groups involved in unlawful activities, discussing their ways, abilities, weaknesses, limits and intentions that could be used for effective law enforcement action.[5]

Analysis

Analysis of either information or intelligence is the unravelling or separation of a thing into its constituent parts, ascertaining those parts, tracing of things to their source to discover the general principles behind them, and a table or statement of the results of this process.[6]

Intelligence Analysis

Intelligence analysis is entirely relating to the gathering and use of information, evaluating it to process it into intelligence, and then analysing that intelligence to produce products that would support informed decision making.[7]

The final objective of intelligence analysis is to develop appropriate inferences that can be acted upon with confidence. In view of this, effective intelligence analysis consists of integrating collected information and then developing and testing hypothesis based on that information through continuous iterations of additional data collection, evaluation, integration, and inductive reasoning. The desired end products are inferences that specify the who, what, when, where, why and how of the activity of concern and lead to the right actions.[8]

The processing of reliable intelligence is the foundation of effective law enforcement. Analysis organises and interprets the intelligence in a way that significantly improves its success in combating organised crime. Analysis identifies and predicts trends, patterns or problem areas requiring action.[9]

Intelligence analysis is the process of applying certain questions, evaluating the answers and choosing how to respond or act. The questions are:[10]

- What exactly is the problem; what decision do we have to make and why is it significant or important?
- What information do we already have or might we reasonably obtain that could be relevant to the problem in hand. Where is it/how can we get it?
- What meaning can we extract from the information; what does it tell us about what is going on?
- Is there only one possible explanation, or are there other alternatives or options. Are some more likely than others?
- How does this affect the decision we have to make, are some options potentially better than others; do some carry greater risk of success and/or failure?
- Are we ready to take action with a reasonable level of confidence, or do we need to gather more information first? If so, what else do we need and where/how can we get it?

Intelligence analysis is first and foremost a thinking process; it depends upon cognitive functions that evolved in humans long before the advent of language.[11] The personal characteristics of intelligence analysts are demonstrated behaviours that reflect thinking and/or the intrinsic drive to think.[12]

Benefits of Critical Thinking in Intelligence Analysis

Thinking is the means through which analysts convert information to intelligence; and it is through critical thinking, the cognitive skills are applied to make the transformation.

Analysts producing intelligence employ the core cognitive skills of critical thinking – interpretation, analysis, evaluation, inference, explanation, and self-regulation.[13] They do not merely state results, they move beyond that to defending procedures, and presenting arguments.[14] Questioning biases and mind-sets encourage consideration of different likelihoods, an example of a critical spirit.[15]

Critical thinking contributes to short-term analysis, and takes on a crucial role in longer-term analysis. Without a doubt, constructing a full picture of a matter or target requires critical thinking to determine which previous reports are included or excluded. "How do the parts contribute to the whole?" and "How is the whole greater than the sum of its party?" are questions analysts ask. When formerly published intelligence reports deviate, the critical thinking process helps the analysts ensure that the deviation is well-thought-out and that the resulting intelligence is not just satisfying the minimum requirements.[16]

Intelligence failures are inescapable if analysts lack critical thinking skills. It is however not the panacea to intelligence failures as they can still be expected,[17] but then again critical thinking will make certain that rightful inferences are drawn from the mass of information the intelligence analyst work with, and therefore reduce intelligence failure to the barest minimum.

Critical thinking in the analysis process minimises the chances of specific failures. Its importance to many parts of the intelligence production process increases the chances of intelligence success. Critical thinking offers structure to the reasoning process that identifies for analysts where they are likely to go off track. It provides a vehicle for self-reflective reasoning that leads to improved thinking.[18]

Important Critical Thinking Skills for Intelligence Analysis

There are basically 11 critical thinking skills that are vital to successful intelligence analysis based on their relationship to the principal intelligence function they serve. The skills are as follows:[19]

Assess and Integrate Information
- *Envision the end state of the analysis* and use that vision to guide and limit the analysis to those tasks most likely to attain the desired

goal, checking on the process and products to ensure movement along the right path.

- *Assess and filter for relevance and validity,* examining information for its potential contribution to the objectives of the analysis.

- *Extract the essential message* by sorting through the details of information to distinguish the essential from the non-essential, and by generating clear, concise statements summarising the main points.

Organise Information into Premises

- *Recognise patterns and relationships,* establishing causes and effects vital to understanding, situations, threats, processes and events during the development of premises in an argument.

- *Challenge assumptions* so as to avoid ideas that might be treated as facts but that are not supported by available evidence or might be related to biases that have been introduced by mind-sets or expectations.

Develop Hypotheses

- *Establish logical relationships* by applying inductive logic to derive one or more hypotheses from the set of premises summarising facts derived from available information.

- *Consider alternative perspectives* by setting aside personal inclinations, values and expectations so as to develop explanations (hypotheses) that cover the full range of possibilities.

- *Counter biases, expectations, mind-sets and oversimplification* by developing the ability to recognise the possible effects of these influences and developing techniques to keep them from distorting the products of analysis.

Test Hypotheses

- *Consider value-cost-risk trade-offs in seeking additional information* to employ available resources in a manner that will produce the greatest value for the resources expended and the time available.

- *Seek disconfirming evidence* during the testing of hypotheses when the more natural inclination is to seek confirming evidence.

- *Assess the strength of logical relationships* in a manner that provides a numerical probability estimate of the confidence one can have in the validity of hypotheses and inferences.

Human Limitations that affect Critical Thinking

One of the biggest limitations to critical thinking in intelligence analysis is human limitations. These are limitations that stem from complexities, biases, uncertainties and domain expertise.[20]

Complexity

The complexity of information to be analysed can rise quickly and without difficulty. The potential scope of complexity becomes obvious with the recognition that it is not unusual for an analyst to address hundreds of thousands of entities. This scenario can pose a major analytical challenge. Types of relationships and unpredictability of conditions also contribute to complexity. In addition, analyst employing a simplification of strategies can lead to biased results like concentrating on vivid immediate cases rather than on more abstract, pale statistical data that are often of much greater value.[21]

Bias

Bias influences the analysis of information in many ways. In intelligence analysis, confirmation bias poses one of the greatest challenges. Confirmation bias is the choosy use of information to back what we already believe, discounting information that would disapprove the belief. Examples of human tendencies that contribute to confirmation bias are:

- Humans tend to perceive what they expect to perceive and, as a consequence, valuable experience and expertise can sometimes work against an analyst when facing new or unexpected information or situations.

- Mind-sets are quick to form but resistant to change, leading analysts to persist with a hypothesis in the face of growing disconfirming evidence.

- Well-established thinking patterns are difficult to change, leading to difficulties in viewing problems from different perspectives or understanding other points of view.[22]

Uncertainty

The intelligence analysts' work is two-pronged – while conducted and surrounded by uncertainty, its aim is to reduce the hanging clouds of uncertainty through which decisions and actions must take place. In view of this, the employment of critical thinking skills is crucial to arriving at the level of confidence one ought to have in the inference.[23]

Furthermore, there are trade-offs the analyst must make – the answers to the questions: Who? What? When? Where? Why? and How? It also includes the level of confidence the inference can get. More details provide a more suitable inference, but naturally at the sacrifice of confidence; less detail provides a greater level of confidence but then naturally at the sacrifice of effectiveness. Making an effective trade-off between detail and confidence is one of the challenges faced by the analysts.[24]

Domain Expertise

The final potential human limitation to critical thinking in intelligence analysis is the lack of domain expertise for the analyst. It is not possible for the analyst to be proficient in all the fields required for a typical analysis. This is where critical thinking skills are expected to compensate for the lack of domain expertise. It is also needed for the development of expertise in domains that are relevant to current and future analysis.[25]

Intelligence-Led Policing

Intelligence-led policing is a management philosophy supporting optimal resource allocation based on a full understanding of the operating environs. It is a philosophy that supports decision makers who seek intelligence to improve their judgement and assist them to make the best possible decisions in relation to crime control strategies, resources allocation and tactical operations.[26]

The intelligence-led policing model has also been referred to as a set of interconnected philosophies, processes, values and methods that enable continuous improvement of the efficiency and effectiveness of operational police work, led by specially designed, selected and structured intelligence. This later becomes the foundation for strategic (long-term) and operational (short-term) decisions. It is also the management of criminal intelligence and planned operational police work, in which intelligence is the foundation when setting priorities, strategic and operational objectives in the suppression of crime and other security threats.[27]

The objectives of intelligence-led policing is to identify and resolve criminal offences and security threats, as well as increasing trust in the police while keeping all the stakeholders satisfied. The model enables an effective an efficient police response to the threats of modern crime in accordance with available resources.[28]

Origins

The term intelligence-led policing originated from United Kingdom. It was first developed as a concept by the Kent Constabulary in response to sharp increases in property – related offences (e.g. burglary and automobile theft) at a period police budgets were being cut. The Kent Policing Model, as it was initially called, referred less serious calls for general non-police services to other agencies, giving it the opportunity to allocate more police time to intelligence units that were created to focus on the main criminal activities. Once crimes and problems are identified and quantified through intelligence evaluation and analysis, it is possible to then target the main actors for investigation and prosecution. Since the persons and groups targeted in Kent were those responsible for major criminal activities, crime was greatly reduced.[29]

Following the September 11, 2001 terrorist attacks in the United States of America, the need for law enforcement agencies to increase their knowledge, develop intelligence, and join forces efficiently to ensure safety became more prominent. This has led to a change of focus among law enforcement agencies from reacting to crime, to collecting and analysing information about crime that will guide efforts in the investigation and prevention of it. Intelligence-led policing focuses on key criminal activities and those that commit it.[30]

Advantages of Intelligence-Led Policing

There are numerous advantages of intelligence-led policing over traditional policing. The main ones are:
1. A proactive approach in combatting crime is the essence of this model. This approach is reflected in a thorough analysis and

assessment of the state of crime and in identifying risks and threats, as well as trends for the future. Crime assessment and prediction for future development is a foundation for police managers when making effective decisions and executing efficient operational police steps and measures. This contributes to noteworthy reductions in criminal activities and enables the police to be a step ahead of criminals.

2. Consistency, non-selectivity and focus on serious criminal offences, which translates to no one being above the law, and that individuals planning and committing serious crimes are the topmost concern of criminal intelligence work.

3. Inter-departmental coordination and cooperation with defined competencies, obligations and responsibilities in the performance of police duties.

4. Inter-agency cooperation and partnership as well as international agencies in combatting crime.

5. Transparent and standard methods of decision making.

6. Focussed gathering of data and information in consonance with well-defined objectives, priorities and needs.

7. An effective management of information and material on crime based on well-defined

standards, procedures and practice of criminal intelligence affairs.

8. A more effective management of police work and risks based on better criminal intelligence.
9. Identification of deterrence methods.
10. Rational use of human and material resources.[31]

Necessary Conditions for Intelligence-Led Policing

Certain conditions are necessary for the effective operation of intelligence-led policing. Key amongst them are:

1. *Leading and Steering* – a key function of the model is the creation of a strategic and operational level that will carry out their duties in accordance with a set methodology and structure of accountability.
2. *Systematised Criminal Intelligence Process* – the entire criminal intelligence process in operation must be structured into sub-processes (tasks), functions and activities that are either mutually related or take place at the same time.
3. *Effective Organisational Structure* – organisational units and sub-units that are engaged in criminal intelligence and police operations are setup in such a way as to be well-suited with clear processes and functions (performance of related processes

and functions within the sane organisational units).

4. *Sources of Data and Information* – identification and effective utilisation of all available open and closed sources with the objective to collect data and information.

5. *Focus on the Most Difficult Security Problems* – that is, organised crime, corruption and other serious criminal offences, as well as their perpetrators.

6. *Criminal Intelligence Products* – in accordance with the well-defined methods for the performance of criminal intelligence work and defined quality criteria, the creation of criminal intelligence products, which will properly define objectives, and determine priorities and decision making for policing.

7. *Legal Framework* – charting an appropriate legal framework for intelligence-led policing to successfully function.

8. *Human Resources* – special selection of police officers, and provision of requisite training in criminal intelligence.

9. *Technical Resources* – necessary infrastructure: developed data bases and information technology, adequate premises, technical equipment and tools are necessary elements for the successful implementation of intelligence-led policing.

10. *Time as a Resource* – time and patience is needed for a new organisational culture and policing philosophy to work.[32]

Intelligence-Led Community Policing

Intelligence-led policing is philosophically close to community policing as a crime fighting philosophy, while also retaining its dissimilarities. In its original formulation, intelligence-led policing could be considered incompatible with the doctrines of community policing philosophy – community contact and empowerment. Where community policing lays emphasis on policing to the needs and desires of the local community, intelligence-led policing is a process whereby strategy and priorities are determined through a more objective analysis of the criminal environment. Community input, while often sought, is not an indispensible element in intelligence-led policing, but remains a principal information source.[33]

Intelligence-led policing works in tandem with community policing. Where community-oriented policing lays emphasis on policing to the needs and desires of the local community, intelligence-led policing uses processed information, i.e. data analysis and criminal intelligence, as the fundamental basis for an objective, decision-making framework that facilitates crime prevention, reduction, disruption and dismantling through both strategic management and effective enforcement strategies targeting serious crimes and/or prolific offenders.[34]

In general, while the key objective of community policing is to increase collaboration with members of the public and their perceptions of police legitimacy to pre-emptively address crime and disorder, that of intelligence-led policing is to make the most of data and intelligence from the community and other agencies to more efficiently, effectively and pre-emptively deploy police resources to address the most severe criminal threats.[35]

The philosophy of community policing is built on the belief that people deserve and have a right to have a say in policing, in exchange for their involvement and support. It is also anchored on the perception that the answers to community problems call for agreeing to the police and the public examining novel means to address community concerns beyond a narrow focus on individual crimes and incidents.[36]

Community policing encourages the public to act as partners with the police in preventing and managing crime as well as other aspects of security and order based on the needs of the community. It recognises that community problems, of which crime is one, require community solutions and support.[37]

Intelligence-led community policing is smart policing. It targets active and persistent criminals and their activities. It also seeks to address the causes of crime and conflict in partnership projects with affected communities. Another feature of intelligence-led community policing is its mobilisation of the majority of law-abiding citizens to work with the police to reduce crime and arrest criminals.[38]

CRITICAL THINKING, POLICE OPERATIONS AND DECISION MAKING

Police officers make critical decisions in the course of operations daily. They try to make the best decisions out of prevailing circumstances. Before delving further into the role of critical thinking in police operations and their decision making process, there is need for a proper understanding of what police operations and decision making entails.

Police Operations

Police operations is defined as the duties, obligations, and actions law enforcement officials carry out in the field.[1] It is a specific policing matter or activity requiring a planned response.[2] In the Nigeria Police Force, operations is coordinated by the Department of Operations. The department is headed by a deputy inspector-general of police, and is saddled with the responsibilities of:
    i.   Planning and organising internal security measures and monitoring the execution of

such security measures in time of emergency.

ii. Direction and coordination of Force policies on crime prevention.

iii. Formulation of Force policies on traffic control.

iv. Planning, coordinating and monitoring of the Force communication network.

v. Reviewing and formulating policies on tactical operation schemes for crime control and prevention.

vi. Periodical inspections of various units for effective implementation of the operational policies of the police.

vii. Planning and coordinating joint operation.

viii. Formulating policies, planning and management of incidents such as disturbance, riots, national disasters, elections and suppression of insurrections.

ix. Formulation and implementation of policies on antiterrorism.

x. Liaison, coordination and interaction with other Directorates of the Nigeria Police Force.[3]

Basic Concepts in Police Operations[4]

Certain concepts and situations define the issues involved in police operations. They include:

- *Appreciation* – a logical process of reasoning, with the objective determining the best course of action in any given circumstance from all the known factors available.

- *Commander's Intent* – a clear, concise directive, verbal or written, that outlines the basic purpose of any given operation. It describes a command authority's desired end-state and thus is the unifying factor for focussing subordinates on what has to be achieved in order to realise the intended outcome.

- *Concept of Operations* – a planning document, informed by strategic direction, which outlines in broad terms the proposed operational activity, the baseline, and intent for all further operational planning.

- *Consequences* – the end result of an event affecting goals.

- *Initiating Direction* – a specific strategic-level direction (verbal or written), issued to a nominated operation commander, which describes the broad concept of an impending major operational activity. The main purpose of which is to formalise initiation of strategic and operational level planning.

- *Likelihood* – the probability of something happening.

- *Major or Special Event* – an event that is considered to be a non-routine operational or security related activity that requires special arrangement.
- *Operation Commander* – a command function (not a rank), who is the police officer in charge of the overall management of an operation, and for generating the commander's intent.
- *Operational Plan* – a detailed single-use plan, which is developed for a particular situation at a particular period in time.
- *Operation Project Plan* – the project plan that establishes what the operation is, the outcomes, the timelines and the resources required to achieve it.
- *Operational Order* – a document that links basic information regarding an event or incident with the structure of the police response and, primarily, the operational resource requirement. The purpose of an operation order is to focus and organise the police response in the direction of specific objectives, by defining how resources are to be deployed.
- *Operational Site Survey* – a detailed security survey and assessment of a venue or location preceding the putting into place of any extra security measures.

- *Planned Operation or Event* – an operation where there has been opportunity and time to formulate strategies, tactics, and likelihoods preceding the anticipation of the operation.
- *Risk* – the influence of uncertainty on objectives. It is every so often measured in consequences and likelihood.
- *Risk Assessment* – the whole process of risk identification, appraisal and analysis.
- *Risk Management* – synchronised actions to direct and control an organisation or process with respect to risk.
- *Standing Plan* – a plan put in place to address ongoing risks in an operational environment (e.g. particular threats, events or operational situations that occur on a regular basis).
- *Task Commander* – a command function (not rank) of a police officer accountable to an operation commander for the command.

Processes in Police Operations

Several processes are fundamental to the successful conduct of a police operation. Principal is: briefing and debriefing, operation policy and planning cycle, the principles of planning, and planning documentation.

Briefing

Briefings dictate the manner and style of an operation. It is responsible for the data needed to direct the deployment of resources. All police officers are duty-bound to be comprehensively briefed on the purpose of an operation prior to their participation.

Briefings are structured according to the needs of the operation. The information, intention, method, administration, risk assessment, communications, and human rights and other legal issues (IIMARCH) model is a briefing structure that is widely recognised and adopted. It is illustrated in the table below:[5]

Information	Operation timeline, location details, brief history (if applicable), evaluated intelligence, partner and community issues, and results of community and equality impact assessments.
Intention	Strategy, tactical plan, available powers and policy.
Method	Tactical plan, available powers, policy, and contingency plans.
Administration	Identity of commanding officers, specific officer duties, operational policies (e.g. protocols, arrest, media), partner responsibilities, duty

	times and locations, briefing times and locations, health and safety, policing style and dress code.
Risk assessment	Individual assessment of all relevant risks.
Communications	Mutual aid command protocols, communications plan, radio equipment and channels, call signs, information for public dissemination, and contact information.
Human rights & other legal issues	Relevant conventions on human rights, rationale for justification of operation and disclosure details.

Every operation is expected to meet key objectives. The main ones are:

- Ensuring the team has embraced the important information contained within the briefing (this can be checked by conducting random knowledge checks to confirm understanding).

- Ensuring individual members of staff understand their responsibility for the allocated task.

- Confirming whether there are sufficient resources to conduct the required tasks (this includes situations where staff may self-brief, for example at remote stations).

Care should also be taken in engagements with the media, non-police personnel or members of the public not to disclose sensitive and tactical information. To achieve this, a checklist should be drawn. Briefings should meet the following criteria:

- Secure to prevent unauthorised access or sensitive information being compromised.
- Concise but adequately detailed to comprehensively inform.
- Effectively timed.
- Consistent, especially where large number of officers are involved.
- Documented as part of an operation audit trail.[7]

Debriefing

This is the procedure of evaluating the results and processes of an operation to enrich the knowledge and proficiency of the personnel involved. The purpose of debriefing is to be acquainted with the good practices, flaws, and areas for improvement.[8]

Debriefing should under no circumstances be ignored, no matter the pressures of the operation. The structure of the debriefing begins from the initial stages of the operation to enable deployed personnel at the preliminary phases provide information for the later phases of the police response.[9]

Operation Policy

This is what defines how police officers are duty-bound to operate in practice. It advises on capacity needs, how to employ and manage resources, how to deal with risks, and how the operational objectives would be attained.[10]

The operational policy centres on creating functional operation plans. It is informed by higher order direction and strategic planning. It establishes 'what' is required (task) and 'why' (purpose) of an operational activity; and varies in scale, resolve and duration. The policy also calls for a constant appraisal and assessment and must be sufficiently flexible to agree to changes without muddling it up. It is also an all-encompassing process, based on established project management principles that give room for accountability.[11]

The Operation Planning Cycle

This is a flexible process that enables adaptation to different operational necessities, characteristics and circumstances. Members of operational planning teams must have prior experience in operational planning, or have undertaken training courses directly related to the role of an operational planner, or have embarked on such training upon joining an operational planning team. The activities listed within each phase of the planning cycle must be considered, but not necessarily carried out. There are as follows:

- *Planning Initiation* – this phase of the cycle considers the following objectives: identifying/engaging with the nominated operation commander; identifying/confirming the operational intent, scope and objectives that the proposed operational planning activity will be informed by/addressed; identifying information and intelligence needs; identifying and establishing a core operation planning team equal to the scope and size of the proposed operational activity; identifying and starting preliminary engagement with relevant police functional areas and stakeholder agencies; ensuring a clear and common understanding of planning roles, deliverables and operational planning timelines; carrying out an initial appreciation or risk assessment of the proposed operational activity, identifying supporting administrative requirements and strategies; developing the initial planning document in the form of a concept of operations; and obtaining relevant managerial level approval of the concept of operations.

- *Plan Development* – this phase of the cycle considers the following objectives: endorsement of the initial planning strategies and assumptions as listed in the approved concept of operations; development of comprehensive operational work break-down structures and strategies including specific planning and functional area task-ing, milestones and deliverables (operation project plan); formal and full engagement with relevant police functional areas and external stakeholder agencies; completion of a formal risk assessment and treatment plan; monitoring and reviewing intelligence holdings and any threat analysis summary; conducting operational (not tactical) site surveys; reviewing any relevant external agreements and legislation; identifying and matching resources to operational require-ments (capability, capacity and logistics); incorporating contingencies; utilising the universally accepted command, control and coordination (C3) principles to develop a C3 framework equalling the proposed operational activity; producing operation orders and relevant supporting operational or tactical documentation.

- *Plan Implementation and Execution* – this phase of the cycle considers the following objec-tives: briefing of, and handover to task commanders; finalisation of operational capability and capacity requirements (e.g. training, exercises, rehearsals and logistics);

operational deployment; reviewing and evaluating the operational environment and planning strategies throughout the deployment phase.

- *Planning Finalisation* – this phase of the cycle considers the following objectives: conducting post-operational reviews; reconciling and reviewing any operationally related financial, administrative and logistical support processes/resources; evaluating the entire operation and planning activity (to help future planning/operational activity).[12]

Principles of Planning

This is the process of considering the following 6 basic principles when developing operational plans:

- *Simplicity* – operational strategies communicated in a clear, concise, logical, timely and structured form.
- *Coordination* – effective management of both internal and external resources and personnel.
- *Efficiency* – implementation of effective risk management/appreciation processes to guide the safe and effective utilisation of operational resources.
- *Flexibility* – integration of credible contingencies.

- *Foresight* – anticipation of potentially realistic developments.
- *Security* – consideration of security implications during all stages of the planning process.[13]

Planning Documentation

This is a process that may lead to the development of closely related planning documents such as concept of operations, risk assessments and appreciations, operation orders and standard tactical plans.

- *Concept of Operations* – this is a product of the planning initiation cycle. It is a brief document, structured in the situation, mission, execution, administration and logistics, and command and communications (SMEAC) format, which forms the reference point for all further operational planning. The content outlines the proposed operational activity and includes: the commander's intent with regards to an operation; the complete picture of operational objectives; the proposed approach to realising the objectives; the organisational abilities to effectively execute the proposed operational activity; and how the organisational capacities will be synchronised, integrated into, and support the proposed lead agency or interagency activity. It is highly recommended that the concept of operations is developed by members of the core operation planning team, and progressed once completed through the chain of command for review and approval. Progression to the planning cycle and operation plan development takes place only after the concept of operations has been approved. It is a static document that should never be amended after approval.

- *Risk Assessment and Appreciation* – assessing and managing risk is a vital part of the operational planning process. It enables the operation planner to: establish a reliable and valid basis for decision making and planning, increase identification of opportunities and threats, increase the chances of realising outcomes, effectively allocate and utilise resources, improve operational effectiveness, improve situational awareness and control, institute accountability, ensure operational security, and enhance work, health and safety performance.

- *Operational Order* – the operational order must follow the SMEAC principle in structure. The content of the operational order must also contain the following: current operational situation and organisational objectives; desired operational flow of events; role of each individual/group involved; organisational command, control and coordination (C3) arrangements; means for subordinate commanders translating operational level tasking into any action-orientated (tactical) plans and activities that may be required to effectively support the operation.

- *Standard Tactical Plan* – the standard tactical plan must be approved by the designated operation commander, and may not necessarily form part of the operational level planning documentation. It must also be structured in the SMEAC format and outline the following in specific terms: current tactical situation, objectives and risk environment; step-by-step procedures for the tactical briefing and deployment of members; tactical command structures; logistical requirements and support; mutual assistance arrangements; reporting requirements and communication systems.[14]

Keys to Effective Leadership in Police Operations

To achieve effective leadership in police operations as well as build a successful law enforcement agency, certain principles must form the framework. They include:

- *Defined and Effective Chain of Command* – if there is no defined chain of command, one cannot evaluate the effectiveness of staff.

- *Effective use of Personnel* – the abilities and aptitudes of the officers must be recognised. Assigning police officers to areas where they have demonstrated aptitude, and supporting/empowering them guarantees success.

- *Effective use of Support Personnel* – support personnel must have defined functions. The support functions should not be part of the day-to-day police operations, as they can cause a breakdown of the chain of command and morale among officers. Support personnel, as the name suggests, are in place only to support (not control) the policing function and mission.

- *Effective Supervision* – every supervisor should know what is expected of them. Supervisors and leaders must be empowered to do their jobs. All supervisors should be developed to the same level and provided the same operational educational opportunities. Sending all supervisors to the same leadership schools will help both the leader and the Force build well into the future with a consistent ideology.

- *Build an Effective Training Programme* – training costs money that does not come easily with budgetary constraints consistent with the job. One has to think strategically here. Opportunities can be maximised by sending officers to instructor schools so they can instruct others in the Force at reduced costs. Officers should also be sent to schools that benefit the Force, not the curriculum vitae. Senior officers should coach, train and mentor their subordinates, which is a key function of a supervisor and hold them accountable for lack of performance. There are no shortcuts in training.

- *Defined and Effective Disciplinary Procedure* – this is one of the most important things one can do as a senior police officer. A clearly defined fair-minded process, which corrects behaviour by sanctions as well as training, and in extreme cases gives room for officers to work back into the good graces of the Force, should be developed. Disciplinary issues have to be addressed speedily and impartially, and each violation should be treated as a separate issue that may not be handled the same way. The purpose is to correct behaviours while nurturing subordinates.

- *Defined and Effective use of Resources* – resources (monetary, equipment, personnel etc.) must be prudently and efficiently utilised. Any mismanagement of resources is unproductive and in essence a waste.

- *Effective Programme Development* – development of new, innovative programmes is central to operational success.

- *Utilisation of outside Resources* – police officers in command and leadership positions have to work within their budgetary constraints as well as seek outside support, where such is allowed. Even as a first line supervisor, this should be a priority. There is no open chequebook and police officers must sometimes think outside the box to offer the best services to the public. An example would be forming a good work relationship with local and state governments for logistic support where and when necessary.

- *Most Importantly, take care of the Police Officers* – if one expects police officers to carry out their duties at the level and standards expected, their efforts must be recognised and rewarded. Even the most motivated police officer will fall if he or she feels there is no reward for their efforts. This includes giving them a "clean" and organised area to work. An upgrade of equipment or uniforms can be effective. It is the officers out there who are doing the job, and they can make the Force look bad or good.[15]

Decision Making

To live is to act. To act is to decide. Everyday work and life are an endless sequence of decisions – some of the decisions are minor and insignificant, while some are enormous and life-determining. Critical thinking improves one's decision making abilities by raising the patterns of decision making to the level of mindful and deliberate choice.[16]

As police officers, decision making is a basic characteristic of the job description. This carries along with it a significant weight of appraising tons of data and information, formulating creative options for evaluation, and then ranking and weighing assessment criteria capable of identifying the best decision. Effective officers recognise that decision making is one of those challenges that benefits from critical thinking.[17]

Decision making is closely related and aligned with critical thinking. It is a thought process of selection that lays emphases mainly on making a logical choice from the options that are obtainable.[18] Critical thinking teaches us to think about decisions more carefully, clearly, and rationally.[19] Although decision making does not have to involve critical thinking; critical thinking results in some sort of decision making.[20]

Factors for Critical Decision Making in Policing

Police officers, especially senior ones in command and leadership positions must take correct decisions. The answer to making correct operational decisions lies in the leadership being concerned about doing the right thing for everyone.

Certain considerations have to be taken into perspective when a police officer is considering effective decision making. They include:

- *It is Never about You* – every police officer is duty-bound never to make operational decisions with one's personal wellbeing in mind. There are officers one leads who count on the superior to make the right decision not one that benefits him or her as an individual. Making the best decision that benefits the whole should be the daily objective.

- *Think Globally* – the whole picture must be taken into account when making decisions. Without the whole picture, an informed decision cannot be made.

- *Make the Right Decision for the Right Reason* – every police officer must be ready to make a hard decision even if it may not be popular. Rightful decisions should be made even if it means discipline for your favourite officer or friend. The right thing must always be done.

- *The Needs of the Public/Community can dictate a Decision* – the police is there to protect the citizens. If there are community issues needing to be addressed, decisions have to be made that would yield lasting solutions.

- *Every Decision has a Person Attached to It* – decisions made are like a pebble thrown into a body of water. The ripples are issues that continue to flow outwards and have impact on other things.

- *Do not Judge the Result – Judge the Path to the Result* – police work like results, is sometimes not pretty. A police officer can prepare for every imaginable situation but circumstances will change the situation in seconds and they have to react. Disciplining an officer for a picture-perfect process but not so pretty result, adversely affects not only the officer, but his or her family, fellow officers and the community as well. The focus should be to determine the process the officers used in reaching the result. If it is flawed, it should be revised to make it more effective. The officers should not be punished for it. They did not create the issue, they simply followed directives.

- *Remember the 24-Hour Rule* – the 24-hour rule is simple: When you are angry and make an instant decision it will most likely be ineffective and probably destructive. It is not necessary to wait for 24 hours in most cases, but simply cooling off and gathering all the facts before making the decision.[21]

NOTES

The Concept of Critical Thinking and Policing

1. Egan, Brian Denis, 2005, "The Role of Critical Thinking in Effective Decision Making", *Expert Reference Series of White Papers*, Global Knowledge: available at www.globalknowledge.com [adapted from] *A Brief History of the Idea of Critical Thinking*, available at: www.CriticalThinking.org

2. ____

3. ____

4. ____

5. Dewey, John, 1910, *How We Think*, Boston: D. C. Heath [available online] accessed 2019/9/08.
   ____, 1933, *How We Think: A Restatement of the Relation of Reflective Thinking to the Education Process*, Lexington, MA: D. C. Heath.

6. Butterworth, John, and Thwaites, George, 2013, *Thinking Skills: Critical Thinking and Problem Solving*, Cambridge: Cambridge University Press, Second edition.

7. Bailin, Sharon et.al. 1999, "Conceptualising Critical Thinking", *Journal of Curriculum Studies*, 31 (3): pp. 285 – 302.

8. Schafersman, Steven D., 1991, "An Introduction to Critical Thinking" available at http://www.freeinquiry.com/critical-thinking.html; accessed 9/08/2019

9. Gerras, Stephen J., 2008, "Thinking Critically About Critical Thinking: A Fundamental Guide for Strategic Leaders", [available online], accessed 2019/9/08.

10. Halpern, Diane F., 2014, *Thought and Knowledge: An Introduction to Critical Thinking*, New York and London: Psychology Press, Fifth edition.

11. Bassham, G. et.al. 2011, *Critical Thinking: A Student's Introduction*, New York: McGraw-Hill, Fourth edition.

12. Rowe, Michael, 2008, "What is Policing", quoted from *Introduction to Policing*, (by author), London, Sage [available online], accessed 2019/9/08.

13. Alemika, Etannibi E. O., 2012, "History, Context and Crisis of the Police in Nigeria", in Obi, Comfort and Ekpe, Ferdinand U. (eds), *The Nigeria Police and the Challenges of Policing a Democratic Society*, Abuja, Police Service Commission.

14. Tamuno, T. N., 1970, *The Police in Modern Nigeria*, Ibadan, University of Ibadan Press.

15. Federal Government of Nigeria, 1967, *Working Party Report on the Police and Prisons.*

16. Constitution of the Federal Republic of Nigeria, 1999 as amended.

17. ____
18. Oyakhilome, Fidelis, 2012, "The Law as a Guide in the Performance of Police Duties", in Obi, Comfort and Ekpe, Ferdinand U. (eds), *The Nigeria Police and the Challenges of Policing a Democratic Society*, Abuja, Police Service Commission.
19. Police Act & Regulations CAP. P19 Laws of the Federation of Nigeria 2004.

How to Improve on Critical Thinking

1. Egan, Brian Denis, 2005, "The Role of Critical Thinking in Effective Decision Making", *Expert Reference Series of White Papers*, Global Knowledge: available online at www.globalknowledge.com
2. ____
3. Paul, Richard W and Nosich, Gerald, *A Model for the National Assessment of Higher Order Thinking* (Dillon Beach, CA: Foundation for Critical Thinking, n.d.), quoted in Moore, David T., 2007, *Critical Thinking and Intelligence Analysis*, Washington DC: National Defense Intelligence College.
4. Moore, David T., 2007, *Critical Thinking and Intelligence Analysis*, Washington DC: National Defense Intelligence College.
5. Patel, Deep, 2018, "16 Characteristics of Critical Thinkers," available online at www.entrepreneur.com/article/321660 accessed 10/09/19

6. Bassham, G. et.al. 2011, *Critical Thinking: A Student's Introduction*, New York, McGraw-Hill, Fourth edition.
7. Halpern, Diane F., 2014, *Thought and Knowledge: An Introduction to Critical Thinking*, New York and London: Psychology Press, Fifth edition.
8. www.psychologynoteshq.com/metacognition accessed 17/09/2019

Importance of Critical Thinking in Police Training

1. Sulaiman, Muhammad Abdul, 2017, "Relationship between Learning Styles and Critical Thinking Ability among Trainees of Police Institutions in Nigeria," University of Abuja, unpublished Ph.D. dissertation.
2. Curriculum Advisory Committee to the Law Enforcement Standards Board, 2014, "Law Enforcement Basic Training 720-Hour Curriculum: Competencies and Learning Objectives by Phase," prepared by Training and Standards Bureau, Wisconsin Department of Justice.
3. DuFour, Scot, 2018,"Mastering Essential Police Skills: Critical Thinking and Writing," https://inpublicsafety.com/2018/03/mastering-essential-police-skills-critical-thinking-and-writing/ accessed 20/09/2019.
4. ____

5. Violanti, J. M., 1993, "What Does High Stress Police Training Teach Recruits?: An Analysis of Coping," *Journal of Criminal Justice* 21 (4), 411 – 417, quoted in Barker, Beth A., 2011, "Higher Order, Critical Thinking Skills in National Police Academy Course Development," Capella University, unpublished Ph.D. dissertation.

6. Barker, Beth A., 2011, "Higher Order, Critical Thinking Skills in National Police Academy Course Development," Capella University, unpublished Ph.D. dissertation.

7. McGreedy, K., 1983, "Entry-Level Police Training in the 1980s," *The Police Chief*, 50 (10), quoted in Barker, Beth A., 2011, "Higher Order, Critical Thinking Skills in National Police Academy Course Development," Capella University, unpublished Ph.D. dissertation.

8. Birzer, M. L., 1999, "Police Training in the 21st Century," *FBI Law Enforcement Bulletin*, 68 (7) 16 – 19, quoted in Barker, Beth A., 2011, "Higher Order, Critical Thinking Skills in National Police Academy Course Development," Capella University, unpublished Ph.D. dissertation.

9. Cohen, Marvin S. et.al. 1998, "Critical Thinking Skills in Tactical Decision Making: A Model and A Training Strategy," Arlington, Virginia: Cognitive Technologies, Inc., www.academia.edu/4699849/Critical_Thin

<u>king Skills in Tactical Decision Making
A Model and A Training Strategy</u>
accessed 21/9/2019
10. _____
11. _____

Application of Critical Thinking to Criminal Investigation

1. Suit No: SC: 201/2000 (2002) LPELR –
   SC.201/2000 *Chief Gani Fawehinmi v.
   Inspector-General of Police, Commissioner of Police,
   Lagos and Nigeria Police Force.* Available at:
   <u>www.lawpavilonpersonal.com/newfulllawre
   port.isp</u>?
2. *Foundations of Criminal Investigation.* Available at
   <u>www.pearsonhighered.com/assets/samplec
   hapter/0/1/3/2/0132470920.pdf</u>
3. Suit No: SC: 201/2000 (2002) LPELR –
   SC.201/2000 *Chief Gani Fawehinmi v.
   Inspector-General of Police, Commissioner of Police,
   Lagos and Nigeria Police Force.* Available at:
   <u>www.lawpavilonpersonal.com/newfulllawre
   port.isp</u>?
4. Peterson, Marilyn B., 2005, "An Analytical
   Approach to Investigation," available at
   <u>www.policechiefmagazine.org/an-analytical-
   approach-to-investigation/</u>
5. _____
6. Gold, Rod, and Plecas, Darryl, 2016,
   Introduction to Criminal Investigation: Processes,

Practices, and Thinking, New Westminster, BC: Justice Institute of British Columbia.

7. ____
8. ____

Critical Thinking and Intelligence Analysis

1. Criminal Intelligence: Manual for Analysts, 2011, New York: United Nations.
2. Lowenthal, Mark M., 2000, *Intelligence: From Secrets to Policy*, Washington, DC: CQ Press.
3. Criminal Intelligence: Manual for Analysts, 2011, New York: United Nations.
4. Lowenthal, Mark M., 2000, *Intelligence: From Secrets to Policy*, Washington, DC: CQ Press.
5. Criminal Intelligence: Manual for Analysts, 2011, New York: United Nations.
6. ____
7. ____
8. Harris, Douglas H. and Spiker, Alan, 2012, "Critical Thinking Skills for Intelligence Analysis," in *Ergonomics: A Systems Approach*, Nunes, Isabel L. (ed.), available at www.intechopen.com/books/erggonomics-a-systems-approach/critical-thinking-skills-for-intelligence-analysis
9. http://www.nationalcrimesquad.police.uk accessed 25/09/19
10. Criminal Intelligence: Manual for Analysts, 2011, New York: United Nations.
11. Devlin, Keith, 2000, "The Role of Conceptual Structure in Human Evolution" in

Bernhard Ganter and Guy Mineau (eds.), *Conceptual Structures: Logical, Linguistic, and Computational Issues*, 8th International Conference on Conceptual Structures, Berlin: Springier Verlag.

12. Yu, Chong Ho, 1994, "Abduction? Deduction? Induction? Is There a Logic of Exploratory Data Analysis?" Paper presented at the Annual Meeting of the American Educational Research Association (New Orleans, LA, April 4 – 8, 1994).

13. Facione, Peter A., 1998 (updated 2004), *Critical Thinking: What it is and Why it Counts*, Millbrae, CA: California Academic Press. Available at: www.insightassessment.com/

14. _____

15. Moore, David T., 2007, *Critical Thinking and Intelligence Analysis*, Washington DC: National Defense Intelligence College.

16. _____

17. _____

18. _____

19. Harris, Douglas H. and Spiker, Alan, 2012, "Critical Thinking Skills for Intelligence Analysis," in *Ergonomics: A Systems Approach*, Nunes, Isabel L. (ed.), available at www.intechopen.com/books/erggonomics-a-systems-approach/critical-thinking-skills-for-intelligence-analysis

20. _____

21. _____

22. ____

23. Klein, G. A. et.al. 2006, "Making Sense of Sensemaking: A Macrocognitive Model," *IEEE Intelligent Systems, 21 (5)* pp. 88 – 92.

24. Harris, Douglas H. and Spiker, Alan, 2012, "Critical Thinking Skills for Intelligence Analysis," in *Ergonomics: A Systems Approach*, Nunes, Isabel L. (ed.), available at www.intechopen.com/books/erggonomics-a-systems-approach/critical-thinking-skills-for-intelligence-analysis

25. ____

26. Fuentes, Colonel Joseph R. 2006, *Practical Guide to Intelligence-Led Policing*, New York: Manhattan Institute for Policy Research.

27. Kostadinović, Nenad and Klisarić, Milan, 2017, *Intelligence-Led Policing Handbook*, Belgrade: Ministry of Interior of the Republic of Serbia.

28. ____

29. Peterson, Marilyn, 2005, *Intelligence-Led Policing: The New Intelligence Architecture*, Washington, DC: Bureau of Justice Assistance, available online at https://www.ncjrs.gov/pdffiles1/bja/21068 1.pdf

30. International Association of Chiefs of Police, 2006, *Intelligence Led Community Policing, Community Prosecution, and Community Partnerships*, Washington, DC: Office of Community Oriented Policing Services.

31. Kostadinović, Nenad and Klisarić, Milan, 2017, *Intelligence-Led Policing Handbook*, Belgrade: Ministry of Interior of the Republic of Serbia.

32. ____

33. Wells, Ronald. 2009, "Intelligence-Led Policing: A New Paradigm in Law Enforcement." Available online at www.patc.com/weeklyarticles/intelligencepolicy-pdf

34. United Nations Department of Peace Keeping Operations and Department of Field Support, 2016 (reviewed 2018), *Guidelines on Police Operations*, available online at https://police.un.org/sites/default/files/sgf-guidelines_police_operations-2015.pdf

35. Bullock, K. 2013, "Community, Intelligence-Led Policing and Crime Control," *Policing and Society, 23 (2)*, pp. 125 – 144.

36. Mathias Graham et.al. 2006, *Philosophy and Principles of Community-Based Policing*, Belgrade: South Eastern and Eastern Europe Clearinghouse for the Control of Small Arms and Light Weapons. www.seesac.org

37. United Nations Department of Peace Keeping Operations and Department of Field Support, 2016 (reviewed 2018), *Guidelines on Police Operations*, available online at https://police.un.org/sites/default/files/sgf-guidelines_police_operations-2015.pdf

38. Mathias Graham et.al. 2006, *Philosophy and Principles of Community-Based Policing*, Belgrade: South Eastern and Eastern Europe Clearinghouse for the Control of Small Arms and Light Weapons. www.seesac.org

Critical Thinking, Police Operations and Decision Making

1. https://study.com/academy/lesson/police-operations-theory-practice.html accessed 22/09/19

2. Australian Federal Police National Guideline on Operational Planning, available online at: https://www.afp.gov.au/sites/default/files/PDF/IPS/AFP/2520/National/guideline-on-operational-planning.pdf

3. https://www.npf.gov.ng/aboutus/Force St ructure.php accessed 24/09/19

4. This section is drawn largely from: Australian Federal Police National Guideline on Operational Planning, https://www.afp.gov.au/sites/default/files/PDF/IPS/AFP/2520/National/guideline-on-operational-planning.pdf; Australian Federal Police National Guideline on Risk Management, available online at: https://www.afp.gov.au/sites/default/files/PDF/IPS/afp/national/guideline-on-risk-management.pdf; and Operations: Briefing and Debriefing, available online at:

https://app.college.police.uk/app-content/operations/briefing-and-debriefing

5. Operations: Briefing and Debriefing, https://app.college.police.uk/app-content/operations/briefing-and-debriefing

6. ____

7. ____

8. ____

9. ____

10. Australian Federal Police National Guideline on Operational Planning, available online at: https://www.afp.gov.au/sites/default/files/PDF/IPS/AFP/2520/National/guideline-on-operational-planning.pdf

11. ____

12. ____

13. ____

14. ____

15. Powalie, Anthony 2016, "10 Keys to Effective Police Leadership," available online at: https://www.policeone.com/chiefs-sheriffs/articles/169588006-10-keys-to-effective-police-leadership/

16. The Foundation for Critical Thinking 2012, "Critical Thinking and the Art of Making Intelligent Decisions," A Two-Day Seminar held at Claremont Hotel, near UC Berkeley, California www.criticalthinking.org

17. Gerras, Stephen J., 2008, "Thinking Critically About Critical Thinking: A

Fundamental Guide for Strategic Leaders", [available online], accessed 08/9/2019.

18. Noel, Lovely et.al. 2017, "Critical Thinking, Decision Making and Mindfullness," *Fischler College of Education: Student Articles. 16* https://nsuworks.nova.edu/fse_stuarticles/16

19. Bassham, G. et.al. 2011, *Critical Thinking: A Student's Introduction*, New York: McGraw-Hill, Fourth edition.

20. Kamerer, Jessica and Russ, Tameka 2017 "Critical Thinking and Decision Making Handbook," *Fischler College of Education: Student Articles. 14*

https://nsuworks.nova.edu/fse_stuarticles/16

21. Powalie, Anthony 2016, "7 Factors for Critical Decision Making for Police Leaders," available online at: https://www.policeone.com/patrol-issues/articles/195983006-7-factors-for-critical-decision-making-for-police-leaders/

INDEX

About the Authors

Mathias Okoi-Uyouyo was educated at Mary Knoll College, Okuku – Ogoja, and the University of Calabar. He is the author of several books amongst them: *Yakurr Systems of Kinship, Family and Marriage, M. D. Yusufu: Beyond the Cop, Issues in the Protection and Promotion of Human Rights* (ed.), and *Stepping Forward with Uti J. D. Agba* (with Goddy Jedy Agba). He combines his writing career with a job in the public service, and is presently a Deputy Director with the Police Service Commission.

Abdul M. Sulaiman was educated at Ahmadu Bello University, Police Academy, Nigeria Defence Academy, University of Hong Kong and the University of Abuja. He is a Deputy Commissioner of Police in the Nigeria Police Force. He has held offices as: Police Public Relations Officer, Sokoto State; Head of Criminal Intelligence Bureau, Federal Capital Territory Police Command; Head of Intelligence and Special Operations, as well as Counter Terrorism and General Investigation, Economic and Financial Crimes Commission; Director of Operations, Special Presidential Investigation Panel, and Force Insurance Officer. His collaboration with Mathias Okoi-Uyouyo, *Critical Thinking and Policing* is his first book.